hackerspace

When you think of a hacker, what comes to mind? Neo, from the movie *The Matrix*, living in a tiny apartment and invading government sites for a living? Or the high-profile, expensive devices used in *007 Skyfall*? Actually, hacking doesn't require doing anything illegal; it is just tinkering with computers and systems. In addition, it is a lot easier than it looks: you can learn it in hackerspaces.

hacklabs

You don't have to be a math genius to program computers, build machines and make them do whatever comes to mind. Nowadays, you can find clubs and communities in most cities with collective labs called hackerspaces, places where people can learn to work with computers, machining, technology, science, digital and electronic art, animation, games.

In these places, everyone can be a teacher or student, and you can find people with similar interests to develop cool projects. These places aren't even expensive. Usually, users contribute with a small fee to buy the equipment used by everybody. They also don't have age limits or genre specifications. You don't even need any previous knowledge – just a desire to learn and have fun.

programming language

This is like any other language (such as English or Japanese) but this one allows you to communicate instructions to machines, particularly computers. You can create programs, games, apps, or whatever you want.

where to go?

These are some of the many places where you can learn to program a computer. Check out one of this labs or websites where you can practice online.

Bauru (SP) | Oeste Hacker Clube | (oestehc.com.br/)
Belo Horizonte (MG) | Área31 Hackerspace | (www.area31.net.br/)
Campo Grande (MS) | Sucuri Hacker Club | (www.sucurihc.org/)
Goiania (GO) | Cora Hacker Clube | (www.hackerspacego.org/cora/)
São Paulo (SP) | Garoa Hacker Clube | (garoa.net.br)
São Paulo (SP) | Marialab Hackerspace | (marialab.com.br/)
Porto Alegre (RS) | MateHackers | (matehackers.org/)

Online:
Code (code.org)
Scratch (scratch.mit.edu/)
RodAda Hacker (rodadahacker.org/)

COOL JOBS FOR THE FUTURE

What do you want to be when you grow up? The answer is not simple anymore. Forget the traditional jobs of your grandparents and parents. In the next 10 or 20 years, we will need different jobs for a different world. Check out these big changes and discover what kind of professional you could be.

BACK TO THE FUTURE

If we already depend on technology to communicate and work, in the future most of the objects of our everyday life will be connected to the Internet: car, refrigerator, watch, shower, bed, laundry machine… Computers will command our physical and virtual lives! On the other hand, we will need to learn how to live in a world with higher global temperatures, and a lack of potable water and other natural resources. Another important fact: people will live longer and have fewer children.

NEW CAREERS

Future scenario: It is highly possible that many of us will have a personal "avatar" to work and interact with colleagues in virtual environments, just like if we lived inside a video game.

New job: Virtual-Reality Artist

What does it mean?

This professional will design virtual conference rooms and create special effects for augmented-reality apps, with 3-D images and interaction.

Future scenario: From an airplane to a toothbrush, the basic materials we use today to build the majority of the objects around us are made from steel, iron, and oil. But these natural resources are limited and will become very rare.

New job: Emerging Materials Engineer

What does it mean?

This professional must have a deep knowledge of biotechnology and nanotechnology, the science of working with atoms and molecules. He or she will research and develop new smart materials to reinvent the industry.

Future scenario: The high quality of medicine and medical treatments will help people live many more years than today. The large population of senior citizens will need professional help to stay in good health.

New job: Personal-Care Coordinator

What does it mean?

He or she will be responsible for monitoring the health treatment of the elderly and coordinating the work of nurses and caregivers. He or she will be the best partner of the family, helping them to give their loved ones the best treatment available.

Future scenario: Humans will explore the secrets of the universe and send missions into space to collect materials and resources on other planets. A trip like this will tend to be less expensive and much more common than today.

New job: Aerospace Engineer

What does it mean?

This professional will study and design the next generations of airplanes and spacecraft, including all the parts that go into them. This transportation must be strong enough to withstand high pressure and strong forces.

Volunteer Abroad Programs

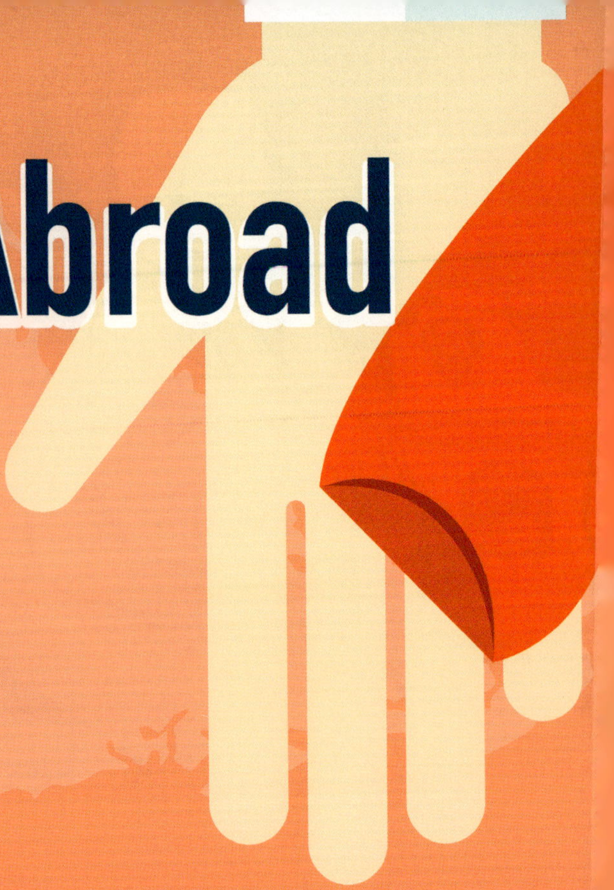

First things first

Before starting, you can search for a good exchange agency in your city. They usually have connections with legitimate organizations that help people overseas.

You can also look for organizations like the Rotary Club or UNICEF and sites like «www.gooverseas.com», «amigosinternational.org» or «goabroad.com». They offer endless links to different companies that sponsor volunteers wishing to go abroad. They also provide an idea of the different possibilities and the basic price range for the fees.

Help kids or the environment

There are lots of things you can do, depending on your interests. You can work with childcare, community development, outdoor construction, sports, art, music, or even work on an organic farm. You can take care of animals and help with preserving the environment. You can also choose a faraway place or somewhere near home. The choices are almost endless!

School vacations are an opportunity to get out and do something different with your time. Instead of watching movies and playing video games, you can go and volunteer in a foreign country. It is an excellent opportunity to learn a foreign language, get to know new cultures, travel to exciting places and make new friends. And, best of all, you will be helping people.

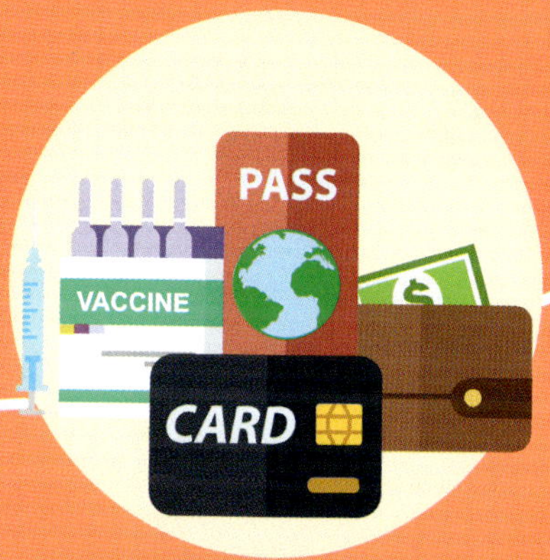

What do you need?

- You will need your parents' authorization if you are under 18;
- You may need vaccines, depending on the country you want to visit;
- You will need a passport and, sometimes, a visa;
- You will need some money for tickets and expenses;
- You will need basic English language skills and, sometimes, to know some basic words and expressions in the native language of the place you are going to work.

Do I have to pay to work?

Volunteering abroad is almost never completely free and cheaper programs offer less support for foreigners than you might actually wish you had. The website «www.moneycrashers.com» offers information on how to organize your research into which program to pick and how exotic of a program you can handle.

Some companies specialize in making volunteering more affordable. Love Volunteers offers 120 different options of places to go around the world for safe and rewarding volunteer experiences. And there's more! One interesting option for teenagers during their July school vacations is to go to China and help teach at the summer camps for children. This program costs 180 dollars, which covers housing, meals, and transportation.

99 PROBLEMS

Have you ever been in one of these situations?

- **You go to a store and ask about the price of a camera and the clerk asks to speak to your dad instead.**
- **You wanted to be part of your school math team, but your teacher only asked the boys to join in.**
- **You tell a girl or a boy you like them and they laugh at you.**
- **You have a biology test tomorrow and you still don't understand the subject.**

Situations like these might make us feel uncomfortable, sad or even angry. But you are not alone: everybody, whether they be a child, a teen or an adult, has to deal with problems every day. Rather than ignore them or get anxious about them, you can try these tips for solving problems:

DON'T PANIC!

Identify the problem

1

Try to put into words what exactly the problem is. Focus on the issue, not the person or the emotion. Describe what is causing the problem and what its consequences are. Example:

"I didn't learn anything in biology class in the last two months. I wasn't paying attention in class because I never liked biology. But I need to learn it to finish the school year."

Think of possible solutions

2

List possible solutions for your problem. Example:

"List of solutions:

*Study hard all day and all night untill the test instead of sleeping;

*Ask my friend Mike to help me study;

*Ask the teacher to postpone the test."

List pros and cons of solutions

3

Think about positive and negatives aspects of each solution and make a list. Decide on the most promising solution. Example:

"The teacher won't postpone the test without a good reason. If I ask a friend to help me I won't lose any sleep and learn the subject."

If you haven't been able to find a good solution, go back to Step 2. It might help to talk to other people, like your parents or friends.

Put your solution into action and evaluate

4

Now it's time to act. Afterwards, check to see if your solution worked. If not, think why it didn't work, go back to Step 2 or 3, and start all over again. This time you'll probably do better because now you have more experience. Example:

"I asked Mike to help me study but he said he couldn't. Maybe I should have offered to pay for his help or asked an older student."

Tips on Saving Money

It is a great feeling to have enough money in your pocket to be able to buy what you want. If you find the money you have is not enough to give you this feeling, there are lots of things you can do.

One great money-saving tip is to stop eating at fast-food places. Although these restaurants are not terribly expensive, the amount adds up over time. Taking the time instead to make a bag lunch at home will save you money and make you a healthier person.

You can save money by reusing instead of buying. You can create gift boxes and paper to wrap your gifts out of cool magazine pictures, folded toilet paper tubes, cereal boxes, and more. The online site «pinterest.com» is filled with simple craft ideas that can serve as gifts you can give and even sell! Instead of throwing out your old jeans, you can cut them up and make everything from a blanket to a pencil case.

You can save money if you are making money. You can use your talents and tutor neighborhood kids who need help, offer your time as a babysitter to parents who need a break, or help an elderly neighbor with housework and repairs in exchange for some spending money.

Taking a vow not to watch so much television will save you money in ways you do not normally expect. Turning off the TV saves your electricity bills, but it also limits the amount of time you spend looking at those advertisements that make you want to buy things you really don't need. You can use that time you would have spent watching TV to focus on ways to make money or having friends over for a meal you cooked!

Human beings, among the smartest of the animals on the planet, have extremely well-developed brains to help out with their survival. The sense of smell helps us differentiate between expensive perfume and bug spray, rotten meat and delicious grilled steaks and clean clothes and dirty clothes, all while our eyes are closed!

SMELL

People can even smell fear and disgust. Some studies would even say we can detect trillions of different smells. This helps inform us not to eat things that have just started to go bad, at one end of the scale, all the way up to helping us fall in love with that special someone who smells so good!

Bears have the best noses of all land animals. Their noses are 5 times the size of human noses and can smell things up to 20 miles away. If you camp in the forest, you need to be sure to wrap your food in smell proof containers!

One to two thirds of a shark's brain is dedicated to its sense of smell. Sharks smell blood so well that they can sense just one drop in 25 gallons of water. Just like in the movie *Jaws*, nobody is safe from a shark if they bleeding in the water.

Dogs can smell a spoonful of sugar dissolved in an Olympic pool, and even cancer cells on a person, helping save their lives. Because dogs have such a great sense of smell, we use them for tracking in the forest and finding drug smugglers in airports.

DIY Summer Fun

Anyone can have fun anytime and everywhere with anything. Your backyard, a neighborhood sports court, a club or even your street could be the perfect place to enjoy free time with friends by playing games made from simple and cheap materials. Summer vacations are the perfect time to get active. Curious? DIY!

Water Balloon Dodge Ball

How to play: Divide your friends into two teams and give them the same number of water-filled balloons. Each team has half of the delimited space to hit the others with the water balloons. The winning team is the one with the last person to get hit!

Lawn Twister

How to play: If you don't have the indoor version of the game, you can play the outdoor version just by using four different colors of spray paint and making four rows of five circles on the lawn. As an alternative to the spinner, you can write the name of the colors on pieces of paper, put them in a bag and randomly select them.

Water Slide

How to play: All you will need is a long heavy plastic sheet (the size depends on how much space you have). Lay it out on your lawn or another place with grass. Just make sure you place it on a little slope. Secure the borders with camping spikes and start running a hose at the top of the slide or if you have one or more lawn sprinklers, use those. Now you just have to position yourself at the starter of the slide and have someone push you down. You can compete to see who rides the fastest.

Frozen T-shirt Escapade

How to play: It starts the night before the game: if you are going to have four teams, freeze four wet folded T-shirts, each one inside a plastic bag. When the game starts, hand a bag to each team and shout GO. They have to try and break the ice off the T-shirt to put it on a member of the team. Whoever finishes first wins.

Fish for Marbles

How to play: You will need a small kiddie-sized plastic pool filled with water, ice, and marbles. Each person has to stand in the freezing cold water and fish out the marbles with their toes. Whoever collects the most marbles in two minutes wins!

ATTITUDE on the walls of the city

Do you like art, colorful paintings, and cool writing? If the answer is "yes," maybe you don´t need to spend any money to enjoy all these things in a museum. The walls of the city are full of these kinds of images. Graffiti, for example, is one of the most famous expressions of what we call "street art."

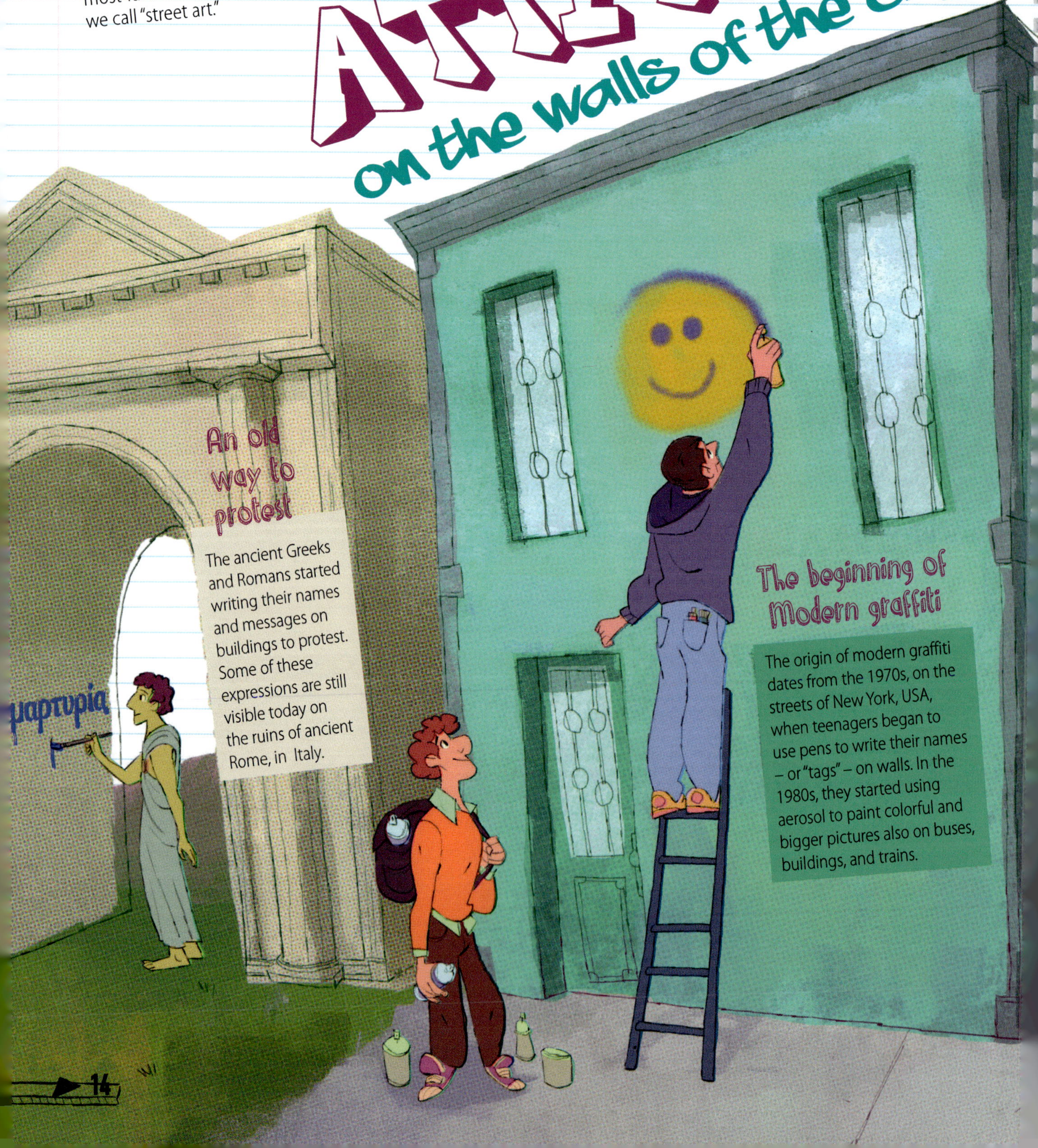

An old way to protest

The ancient Greeks and Romans started writing their names and messages on buildings to protest. Some of these expressions are still visible today on the ruins of ancient Rome, in Italy.

The beginning of Modern graffiti

The origin of modern graffiti dates from the 1970s, on the streets of New York, USA, when teenagers began to use pens to write their names – or "tags" – on walls. In the 1980s, they started using aerosol to paint colorful and bigger pictures also on buses, buildings, and trains.

Famous Brazilian Artists

Eduardo Kobra

His eye-catching work on the streets of São Paulo are unmissable. His style is characterized by rainbow-colored portraits and some vibrant 3-D pictures.

Os Gêmeos

The twin brothers Otávio and Gustavo Pandolfo are famous worldwide for their creative yellow-skinned characters inspired by hip-hop culture. They are invited to paint walls in many cities and also to show their work inside museums.

Speto

São Paulo is also the setting for the beautiful paintings of Speto. The artist looked for inspiration in "cordel literature," a traditional and popular way of telling stories through verses and illustrations.

graffiti styles

Tags – These are a coded version of the writer's name, like their initials. They were used to mark territories in the neighbors of a city. Usually, they had only one color.

Throw-ups – More complex and unique than tags, they include bubble letters, different colors or other mixed styles.

Wheatpaste poster – Posters that are stuck up on walls using a glue made from a mix of flour and water.

Pieces – Very large paintings, usually with 3-D effects and made of a variety of colors.

Stencil – Image or text that is easily reproducible when transferred from a template to a wall through the use of spray paint or roll-on paint.

LET'S HAVE FUN

Quiz

ARE YOU AN OUTGOING PERSON?

ANSWER THESE QUESTIONS AND ADD THE NUMBER OF POINTS FOR EACH ANSWER.

1. Which do you prefer?

(3 points) Group work.

(1 point) Individual work.

(2 points) You work well in both cases.

2. When you are working in a school group, you:

(3 points) Take the lead and tell the others what to do.

(2 points) Try to make everyone agree with one another.

(1 point) Avoid stating your opinion.

3. What do you prefer to do on weekends:

(1 point) Stay home watching movies or playing video games.

(2 points) Hang out with you family for a while or ask a friend to come over.

(3 points) Go out \ hang out with friends.

4. If you need to say something to someone, you rather:

(1 point) Write them a message or an e-mail.

(3 points) Talk to them face to face.

(2 points) Call them on the phone.

5. Where would you rather go?

(2 Points) A movie theater.

(1 point) A deserted beach.

(3 points) A rave.

6. If you are at a party and you don't know anybody, you:

(2 point) Stay in a corner until someone comes and talks to you.

(3 points) Start to talk to the closest person.

(1 points) Leave.

7. Which would you rather be?

(3 points) An actor \ actress.

(2 points) A lawyer or a teacher.

(1 point) An engineer or a painter.

8. People usually say you are:

(3 points) Fun.

(1 points) A good listener.

(2 points) Sweet.

9. When someone says something you don't like, you:

(3 points) Yell at them.

(1 point) Cry.

(2 points) Try and talk to them.

Results:

If you scored less than 13 points, you are an introvert. You probably have a few close friends and don't like to talk or be in social situations. That isn't a problem if your shyness doesn't prevent you from doing things you want to do.

If you scored between 14 and 20 points, you might be what we call an ambivert, a person who has both extrovert and introvert qualities. You probably are a bit shy, but it doesn't get in your way.

If you scored 21 points or more, you're probably very outgoing. It's a good thing for artistic performances or talking in public, but watch out! People might think you show off too much.